A Note to Parents

Dorling Kindersley Readers is a compelling new program for beginning readers, designed in conjunction with leading literacy experts, including Dr. Linda Gambrell, President of the National Reading Conference and past board member of the International Reading Association.

Beautiful illustrations and superb full-color photographs combine with engaging, easy-to-read stories to offer a fresh approach to each subject in the series. Each *Dorling Kindersley Reader* is guaranteed to capture a child's interest while developing his or her reading skills, general knowledge, and love of reading.

The four levels of *Dorling Kindersley Readers* are aimed at different reading abilities, enabling you to choose the books that are exactly right for your child:

Level 1 for **Preschool to Grade 1**
Level 2 for **Grades 1 to 3**
Level 3 for **Grades 2 and 3**
Level 4 for **Grades 2 to 4**

The "normal" age at which a child begins to read can be anywhere from three to eight years old, so these levels are intended only as a general guideline.

No matter which level you select, you can be sure that you are helping your child learn to read, then read to learn!

DK

A DORLING KINDERSLEY BOOK
www.dk.com

Project Editor Penny Smith
Art Editor Susan Calver

Senior Editor Linda Esposito
Senior Art Editor Diane Thistlethwaite
US Editor Regina Kahney
Production Melanie Dowland
Picture Researcher Cynthia Frazer
Jacket Designer Dean Price

Reading Consultant
Linda B. Gambrell, Ph.D.

First American Edition, 2000
2 4 6 8 10 9 7 5 3 1
Published in the United States by DK Publishing, Inc.
95 Madison Avenue, New York, New York 10016

Published in Great Britain by Dorling Kindersley Limited.

Library of Congress Cataloging-in-Publication Data
Chancellor, Deborah
    Holiday! Celebration Days around the World / by Deborah Chancellor.–
1st American ed.
    p. cm. -- (Dorling Kindersley readers)
    Summary: Describes special events from around the world
with the history and traditions that make the holidays memorable,
such as Chinese New Year and Valentine's Day.
    ISBN 0-7894-5710-5(hc) -- ISBN 0-7894-5711-3 (pb)
    1. Special events--Juvenile literature. 2. Holidays--Juvenile literature.
[1. Holidays. 2. Special days.] I Title II Series.

GT3405 .C53 2000
394.26--dc21
                                    99-087063

Color reproduction by Colourscan, Singapore
Printed and bound in China by L.Rex Printing Co., Ltd.

The publisher would like to thank the following for their kind permission to
reproduce their photographs:
Key: t=top, a=above, b=below; l=left, r=right, c=center,
Barnaby's Picture Library: Alistair Bruce 14br; BBC Photograph Library:
13br; J L Charmet: 11tl; Christie's Images: 23a; Corbis: Lyn Hughes
10bc; Et archive: 22br; Image Bank: 20a; Barnabas Kindersley: 15bl,
15acr, 15bcr, 21cr; Mary Evans Picture Library: 28bl, 31tl; Pictor
International Ltd: 8–9b; Powerstock/Zefa: 6ac, 28a; Robert Harding
Picture Library: A Autenzio/Explorer 29b; Telegraph Colour Library:
19a; Tony Stone Images: Jerome Tisne 6br, 16–17b

DORLING KINDERSLEY *READERS*

BEGINNING
TO READ ALONE
2

Holiday!
Celebration Days around the World

Written by Deborah Chancellor

DK

DORLING KINDERSLEY PUBLISHING, INC.
www.dk.com

Fun around the world

Throughout the year
people remember
special days.

They like
to welcome in
the Chinese
New Year.

They like to thank
their mothers
for taking care of them.

They like
to dress up and
scare people
on Halloween.

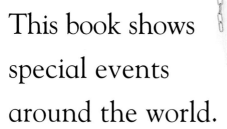

This book shows
special events
around the world.

And it tells us
what makes them
days to remember.

Chinese New Year

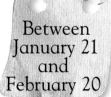
Between
January 21
and
February 20

The Chinese New Year
begins when there is
a new moon in the sky.

This means that it starts
on a different day each year.

Bouncing baby

The Chinese year 2000
is the year of the dragon.
Babies born in 2000
should be strong
and energetic!

Children dress up
in red silk clothes.
In China,
red stands
for happiness.

They are given
"lucky money"
in red and
gold envelopes.

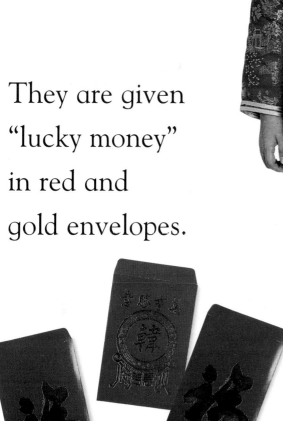

In cities around the world
merrymakers fill the streets.
Dragon dancers weave
in and out of the crowds.

They collect money and lettuce.
Lettuce is a symbol of new life.
The dragon stands for
long life and riches.

Valentine's Day

On Valentine's Day
people send gifts and cards.
These gifts and cards let others know
that they are loved.

The story of Valentine began
when a Roman emperor
banned men from marrying.
He wanted them
to join his army instead.

St. Valentine
was a priest
who carried out
weddings in secret.
He was sentenced
to death.

On his last day he thanked
his jailer's daughter
for her friendship.
He signed his note,
"love from your Valentine."

Today, some senders
do not say who
the gifts are from.

April Fool's Day

This is the day
when people play
tricks on each other.
April Fool's Day
began in France.

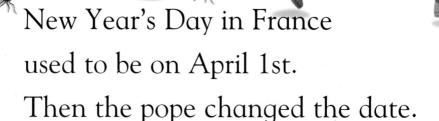

New Year's Day in France
used to be on April 1st.
Then the pope changed the date.

Some people did not know and
kept using the old date.
They were laughed at and
called "April fools."

Sometimes, newspapers and
T.V. programs trick people.

For example, spaghetti is made
from flour, eggs, and water.
But one year a T.V. program
showed spaghetti growing on trees!

spaghetti

Mother's Day

Second Sunday in May

About 100 years ago an American woman named Anne Jarvis asked her friends to wear white carnations to church.

She wanted them to think of her mother, who had died.

Mother's Day in Europe
American soldiers took Mother's Day to Europe during World War II. They sent gifts home on Mother's Day.

Today Mother's Day takes place
on different days around the world.
In the U.S. it is in May.

People give
their mothers
presents and cards.
Children help with
household chores.

Father's Day

Another American,
Louise Smart Dodd,
was the first person
to celebrate Father's Day.

When her mother died,
her father had to bring up
six children on his own.

Roses are the flowers
for Father's Day.
People wear a red rose
if their father is alive
and a white rose
if he has died.

On Father's Day
children send cards
to their fathers.

Halloween

Long ago people
believed that the dead
came back to life on Halloween.

Now people remember Halloween
by going to parties
or trick or treating.
They dress up as ghosts
or scary skeletons.

Then they knock on doors
and play tricks on anyone
who does not
give them treats.

*Candy is often
given at
Halloween.*

Apples ripen in the autumn
so they are used
in lots of Halloween games.
Sometimes players bob for apples
in big buckets filled with water.

Sometimes they bite at apples hung on string. The first person to bite an apple is said to be the first to marry the next year!

Diwali

Hindu is a religion
in which people worship many gods.
There are many Hindu writings
about the adventures of these gods.

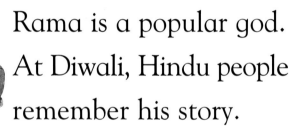

Rama

Rama is a popular god.
At Diwali, Hindu people
remember his story.

Rama was once driven
from his kingdom
by a wicked demon.
The demon kidnapped
Rama's wife, Sita.

Rama and his wife Sita

Rama fought a fierce battle.
He won back his wife and
returned to his kingdom in triumph.

The elephant god
Ganesh is another Hindu god.
Ganesh's father cut off
his son's head by mistake.
He put an elephant's head
in its place.

People decorate their houses
with twinkling lights
called divas.
These lights
are meant
to guide
Rama home.

They also decorate floors in their houses with patterns called rangoli. These are to welcome visitors.

People give each other cards and sweets at Diwali.

Christmas

December
25

Long, long ago
Jesus Christ was born in a stable.
Christians around the world
mark this event with Christmas.

Children put on nativity plays
to tell the story of the birth.

People give each other
presents and cards.

Families decorate
fir trees at Christmas.
These evergreens
are a symbol of
everlasting life.

Many children believe
Santa Claus brings presents
the night before Christmas.
He is said to ride on a sleigh
pulled by reindeer.

The first Santa Claus

"Santa Claus" comes from
the Dutch word for St. Nicholas.
This saint was a rich bishop
who used his wealth
to help poor people.

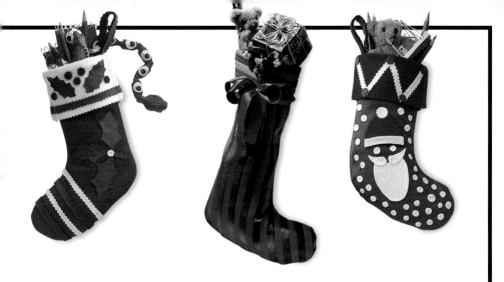

He climbs down chimneys
and fills stockings
with presents for children.

Kwanzaa

December 26 to January 1

This means "first fruits."

At Kwanzaa, African Americans celebrate the harvest in Africa.

Plantain   *Okra*   *Cassava*

They think of their dead relatives as well as the African way of life.

African girl

Forced to America

Africans were taken
to America as slaves.
They were put in chains
and packed onto
crowded slave ships.

Sweetcorn

Yam

Sweet potato

Kwanzaa lasts
seven days.
Each day people
light candles.
They feast
and give presents.

American boy

31

More days to remember

Every year a spectacular carnival
takes place in Rio de Janeiro, Brazil.
Samba schools join a huge parade.
They show off new dances and costumes.

St. Patrick's Day celebrates the life
of the patron saint of Ireland.
In some cities green beer is served and
rivers are even dyed green!

In Japan, Hina Matsuri
is a day dedicated to dolls.
Dolls take away bad luck
when they are cast out to sea.

At the Indian festival of Holi
people cover each other
with bright powder paint.
This celebrates the god Krishna
and how he soaked
his companion Rada
with colored water.

People think about new life at Easter.
Chocolate eggs are popular –
in Australia an enormous egg
weighed as much as ten horses!

Hanukkah is the Festival of Lights.
It is when Jewish people remember
how the Temple of Jerusalem was cleansed.
A candle is lit each night at Hanukkah.